The Art of Small Talk

How to Master the Unwritten Code of Social Skills, Improve Your Charisma, and Little-Known Hacks to Connect with Anyone Effortlessly

I0090405

JASON MILLER

Jason Miller

TABLE OF CONTENTS

Jason Miller

Introduction

At some point in our lives, we have all been that socially awkward person. And whether you have come to label yourself as an introvert, or you are an extrovert who is struggling to connect with that inner social butterfly, we have to come to that place where we realize that social interaction with our peers is essential for human growth.

That said, many of us find it difficult to interact with humans. There are a lot of explanations for this, but this time around, I encourage you to stop giving in to those explanations and instead take a stand today to become better at conversations. It is going to be a scary journey, especially for those of us who are shy and reclusive, but that doesn't have to define you going forward. In this book, you can learn how to take charge of your social life and find ways to build relationships that will not only empower and sustain you, but they will nourish you in ways that you didn't think was possible.

Approach this book with an open mind. Let go of any preconceived notions you have about why you are the way you are. As I said earlier, you may have come to put a label over yourself, and what this does is to help you cope better with the distance you have with the people in your life. However, as humans, we are biologically programmed to seek out each other. There is a longing on the inside of you. Something that wants you to reach out and connect. This is perfectly normal. In this book, I share with you my journey to becoming an extrovert. Now, I use the label 'extrovert,' not because I am the typical definition of someone who enjoys being in crowds. I am reflecting on how I left the place where it was difficult for me to even establish eye contact to this point where I can meet a complete stranger, smile and start a conversation. These are milestones that I crossed, and while it was hard at first, I can tell you that over time, it got easier.

If you are planning on becoming a public speaker, this will provide the foundation or premise for that journey. In this book, you will also learn how to interact with people in a public setting because public speaking is more than just standing on stage and talking to the crowd. You have to connect with them, and while it is a lot easier to connect with people when you are in a one-on-one setting, it is not impossible to replicate that effect in a group setting. And that is just one of the many things you are going to learn in this book. So, as you flip to the next chapter, take a deep and positive breath, let go of your fears, and what you think you can or cannot do. Make your mind a blank slate because here on out, we are writing new experiences in your social life and we are going to do it in style.

So, turn over and let us begin.

Chapter One

Why is it Hard for You to Talk to People?

Before we start reeling out a three-point solution to the problem at hand, it is important to get to the root of the problem first of all. And to get to the root, we seek to answer the questions of why we are the way we are. The better understanding you have about why you act the way you do, the more effective you become at implementing the solutions. More than that, knowing the root of the problem gives you deeper insight into your personality and helps you make sense of the world around you.

Why is it Scary to Talk to People?

If we are going to look into all the reasons explaining why talking to some people might seem like a scary experiment, we will be here until 12 Sundays from now, and we still would not have exhausted half of those reasons. To save us from that stress, I will focus on just one reason. And that reason is very simple; we project our perception of ourselves on other people. Let me explain that.

When we try to talk to people (and by 'we' here, I am talking about us shy folks), we think of how they would react towards us. Before we meet people, we have a certain image of ourselves when it comes to how we look and how we sound. And often, we feel that these perceptions do not match up to the required social standards.

And so every time we meet new people, we feel that they are judging us based on these opinions we have about ourselves. In other words, we think for people when we come across them. And then, on top of that, we insert our negative opinions about ourselves into those thoughts that we are thinking on behalf of those people.

Do you realize how ridiculous that sounds? But that is essentially what we do, and because we think that people are thinking these things about us, it makes it difficult to approach them. These thoughts are not always self-conceived. As in, we do not just sit down and create those thoughts. More often than not, these are things that have happened based on experience. Probably in our childhood, we had a social setting where we were embarrassed by our peers who brutally capitalized on our insecurities. Or perhaps, our parents may have directly or indirectly sowed the seeds of self-doubt in our hearts and we grew up with this unpleasant notion about ourselves.

Another possible root for the negative opinions we have about ourselves could be from the kinds of content that we feed our minds. There are a lot of books, magazines and content out there in the world telling us how we should look. And when we are different from these things, we develop insecurities about those differences. Our fear of talking to people comes from a place of insecurity and to get over it; we would first need to get over ourselves.

Where Does Fear Come From?

Fear is a biological response to anything that threatens your being. When you are afraid, the fear that you experience triggers a survival instinct bent on preserving you. So, if your fear is activated when you get into a social setting, essentially, your mind or brain is trying to preserve you from any perceived dangers in your environment, and this happens because your brain has come to look at social settings as a place that threatens your well-being. This is not something you were born with. It is something that is emphasized over time, like a habit.

Fear is not the horrible monster we have come to know. We may not be like how it makes us feel, but if you look at fear from an objective perspective and get an understanding of it, you would realize that you can harness it for your own good. Fear keeps you alert. Now, when you indulge in fear for too long, you become paranoid. However, if you are able to plug yourself into the root of your fear, you can use that

Jason Miller

knowledge to empower yourself and what do I mean by this?

Since we now know that fear in social settings is triggered because your mind has been conditioned to think that you are being threatened every time you get into a social situation, you can now work out a process of reprogramming your mind to think the opposite. This is not something that is going to happen overnight, as it would require deliberate effort on your part. However, with the commitment, you can make it happen.

I should point out here that for a small group of us, the fear that we experience when we get into social situations is part of our biological makeup and I cannot fully go into the details of that here. This because it is something that will require collaboration with your doctor if you fall under that spectrum. That said, there are still tips you can pick up from this book along the way. I believe that biological makeup or not, there is a psychological angle to this and that is what we want to tackle in this book.

Mental Barriers to Talking to People

Have you ever been in a situation where you finally walk up the courage to talk to a person only to find yourself paralyzed completely on the spot? Even after you spent days to rehearse your lines and conversations, the moment it gets to that point where you were supposed to step onto the plate, you lose it and have that deer caught in the light situation. It is not pleasant. I can tell you for sure because I have been in that boat and there are a lot of reasons for it. Most of which have to do with fear, but seeing as we have already talked about fear in the previous segment, let us look at other reasons that explain the embarrassing situation.

1. Insecurities

We touched on this area earlier when we first started out this chapter. And we are discussing this here because this is a major contributory factor to the mental barriers we experience in our attempts at social interaction. When we try to initiate conversations with people, we are often focused on who we think we are. To make matters worse, we have negative opinions about who we are and this acts as a block in our ability to talk with people.

2. Assertion of Assumptions

When we meet a person, based on certain poor analysis like how the person dresses, the way they talk and so on, we judge them. And based on this judgement, we react. What we have done here is basically to assert an assumption that we have about the person. This causes conflict in conversations because we are unable to get past this mental opinion that we have generated about this person. There is a common phrase that says," do not judge a book by its cover." Many of us take a look at the external attributes of a person without really looking inward to know a person. And without that insight, it is going to be impossible to have a genuine conversation with said person.

3. Language

Language is one of the most complex aspects of human communication. And here, I am looking beyond the differences in our mother and focusing on our perception of what is said and being said to us. Words connote different meanings to each of us and for this reason, we develop different reactions to certain words and phrases. This would explain why certain phases that may have caused a certain group of people to laugh might cause another person to cry. These differences in language can make it difficult for us to talk to people, especially when you consider the fact that shy people are typically very sensitive.

Now that we have set up a premise for why we find it difficult to talk to people, the next course of action is to look into the fears that we face every time we get into a social setting and explore effective ways to overcome it.

Chapter Two

The Foundation of Social Anxiety and Learning to Cope

Social anxiety happens when a person develops a fear of being rejected, judged or negatively evaluated and this feeling of fear is usually brought on or triggered by being in a social setting. The manifestation of social anxiety is usually in one's performance, so in a roundabout way, you can say that social anxiety is performance issues triggered by fear from being in a social setting. If any of this sounds like something you can relate with, you are not alone. Millions of people all over the world suffer from some form of social anxiety or the other. In the next few segments, we will explore the topic in detail and come up with tips on how to maintain high performance even when you are under social pressure due to anxiety.

How to Overcome Social Anxiety

The impact that social anxiety has on our lives is tremendous. However, it does not mean that it cannot be overcome. There are measures you can put in place to help you with the daily steps needed to overcome social anxiety and a lot of these steps are things that you can start doing from your home. That said, it is important to know what spectrum you fall under when it comes to diagnosing a social anxiety disorder. It is a well-known fact that people who suffer from severe and extreme cases would need to rely on drugs and therapy to overcome their struggles. Outside that, these next few steps that I am going to talk about are things that are basically doable from where you are right.

If you have already spoken to your doctor, go ahead and put the steps to practice. Build on it and through it; you can build your esteem enough to help you overcome social anxiety.

1. Confront the situation that triggers your anxiety head-on

It is human to want to immediately take yourself outside situations that cause you to feel a certain kind of way about yourself. However, if you are serious about overcoming anxiety, it is important that you put yourself out there. Just ensure that you do this in moderate and controlled doses. Don't plan on going from being a couch buddy to a cliff jumping adventurer in minutes.

2. Keep a journal

An emotional journal is there to help you keep track of your feelings. That way, you can narrow down the specific emotions that trigger your anxiety. It could be fear, anger or sometimes it could just be activities that take you down memory lane to a negative experience that you had in the past. Knowing your triggers will help you become better prepared

3. Get physical

Physical exercise has a way of making us feel good and better about our bodies, not to mention the fact that it helps you explore your mental headspace and gets you into a positive mindset faster.

4. Let go of any illusions you have about being perfect

Most people who suffer from social anxiety disorder have a problem with performance in public. And that is because they think that people expect them to be perfect. It is impossible to be perfect. Let go of the desire to get people to see you as perfect. It is okay to be you the way you are.

5. Stay positive

Being positive is an essential part of your journey to overcoming social anxiety. Train yourself to stop wandering to the dark and negative recesses of your mind. Focus instead on those things that make you feel good about you as a person and the life that you live.

Advantages of Learning Techniques and Education on Social Skills

Essentially, social skills help to prep you for easy integration into social settings that you are not familiar with. It could be for business purposes or a simple education on how to do certain things when you are in public with people. These things that I am talking about are basically what people consider as proper social skills and it can range from basic conversation to traditionally acceptable interaction based on a specific geography. It is important to learn the skills so that you do not end up offending people.

Beyond that, being knowledgeable of common social skills makes it easier to communicate, as certain social faux pas that may be regarded as disrespectful can quickly earn you the tag of rude or difficult to associate with. And when you have these kinds of tags in social settings, you might as well be wearing the scarlet letter on your forehead. People tend to avoid those that are wearing such tags.

In life, you never know how far you are going to go. You cannot always judge your progression in life based on the people you are associating with you right now. It is possible that in the course of your business or career progression, you could find yourself in some of the most amazing cities and places in the world. Beyond the language barrier which could prevent communication, there are also other things that make interaction in these kinds of settings, and having good knowledge of the social skills tell are peculiar to that region can help you understand what is acceptable and proper.

The Case for Learning About Confidence and Social Skills Together

Knowing the importance of social skills is one thing. Implementing them is another and this is where confidence comes in. A person who is confident in their ability and personality does not let that get in the way of them using the knowledge that they have gained to their advantage. Whether they are in the boardrooms negotiating the next big deal or they are pitching their brands and ideas to potential investors ... or perhaps it's a child speaking up for the first time. Whatever category you fall under, confidence is the key to executing the social skills you have gained in real life.

One way you can go about boosting your confidence is by getting rid of the notion that you are not good enough. I had a counselor who used to tell me that, "if you don't love yourself, how can you expect other people to love you in the same way." It is important to build self-care routines as well as indulge in treats every now and then to help you climb out of that hole of insecurities and self-doubt. You need to begin to take on activities that affirm the many skills that you have to reveal the true personality within and discover people who share the same interests with you. In the next chapter, we will go into more detail about confidence and how to build it. This segment is meant to set a premise for confidence and how it plays out and social interaction.

The combination of being confident and having an understanding of how people interact in a certain setting has a way of portraying us as the ideal person that people should relate with. When people have this kind of perception about you, your social life will experience a massive boost and in my opinion, this is a win-win situation for everyone involved.

Chapter Three

Building Confidence for Better Social Interaction

Confidence, as we have discussed previously, is an essential ingredient for any social interaction; whether you are talking to one single person or a group of three, the right amount of confidence can set the tone for that relationship. You may have heard people use the term "doormats." This usually refers to people who are unable to assert themselves in their relationships and this inability finds its root cause is a lack of confidence. Without confidence, you will not be able to express yourself articulately. And when you are unable to express yourself articulately, people who you are in a relationship with tend to overlook your needs. So, it is important to build one's confidence.

Where Does Confidence Come From?

To put it in very short and simple terms, confidence comes from your own perception of yourself and abilities. In other words, the image or concept you have about yourself is what feeds your confidence. If you have a very poor opinion of yourself, there is a very strong possibility that you will not be a confident person. Confidence has been linked to self-esteem issues and that explains why people with poor self-esteem tend to have poor confidence.

However, while confidence is an innate ability, I would say that the society around you can influence the level of confidence that you have. So if you have people or are surrounded by people who constantly affirm your negative opinion of yourself, this would reduce your self-esteem and in doing so, reduce your confidence. The opposite happens when you surround yourself with people who affirm the positive opinion that you have about yourself. Your confidence level will soar and you find yourself doing amazing things.

Now, some people find it easier to develop confidence. You would find children who are born confident and then you have kids who find it difficult even to maintain eye contact with their peers. Over time, the society that grooms them (which includes their family, their friends, their network at school and outside the school and so on) can determine how far the confidence level of this child goes. That said, if you are struggling with confidence, the first step to building it recognizes that you are more than the opinion that you have about yourself.

The Basic Foundation for Growing the Confidence You Need

The most common tip you get when it comes to building your confidence would be to 'fake it until you make it.' Now, this can come in handy in certain situations. However, it is important to understand that there is a fine line between confidence and arrogance. And if you are faking it, your confidence can sometimes come off as arrogance. Genuine confidence has very little to do with pride or looking down on other people. As I established earlier, confidence is all about who you feel you are on the inside and not about the people on the outside.

If you are constantly putting yourself up against the people in your environment and using that as a yardstick to measure yourself with, you have crossed the line of being confident and entered into arrogance territory. That said, here are some tips on how to grow your confidence;

1. Avoid negative places and people

Nothing pulls your confidence down faster than surrounding yourself with people who are constantly negative. Take yourself out of that environment and find a space that will nurture you positively.

2. Do not accept other people's negative opinion of you

People's notions about you may have been fed by some error or mistake you made in the past but that does not essentially define you. If they insist on identifying you with that negative trait or history, that is their problem. You, on the other hand, do not need to deal with their inability to move past that point.

3. Find your voice

For me, I think that this is the most critical part of developing your confidence. You need to find what is important to you and learn how to voice those needs. You may not have to put it into words right away, but acknowledging to yourself the things that are important to you is a great start.

4. Have a strong support system

Whether it is your family, mentor, or basically people who you often get a positive vibe off, it is important that you build your own village or community of cheerleaders. These are people who genuinely care about your well-being and see the potential that you have on the inside.

Asserting Your Confidence in Social Situations

Before going further in this book, I would like you to ask yourself the following questions; what does confidence look like for you in a social situation? Are you one of those people who feel that talking down or ensuring that your voice is the loudest makes you the most confident? If so, it is time to change that mentality. Confidence is more than just how you appear, although, that also plays a role. However, I feel that appearance and confidence basically stem from being comfortable in outfits that you wear.

A lot of people tend to focus on what they wear (in terms of the designer brand), as well as social status. They also tend to lean on their wealthy background or rich educational history like a confidence crutch of some sort. All this is well and good, but they don't necessarily help your standing when it comes to confidence in a social setting. They may open doors for you, but they will certainly not keep you in the room. Confidence in the social setting is basically learning to speak and while speaking is an essential part of expressing your confidence, listening is just as important. When you feel to listen to people, communication automatically shuts down.

It is for this reason that I firmly believe that in social settings, confidence is a juggling act between speaking and listening at the right and opportune time.

Confidence in communication also extends beyond the verbal aspect. You can use your body language to communicate and confidence can be expressed in your body language. For instance, slouching your shoulders is considered a sign of poor confidence. Also, one's inability to maintain eye contact can be interpreted as poor confidence. And here is my final tip. When next you are given a handshake, ensure that the handshake is firm. That is a nonverbal display of confidence. These tiny attributes are the things that make up what confidence looks like in social interactions.

Chapter Four

Understanding the Mechanics of Human Interaction

Humans are biologically programmed to seek out each other's company. No matter how much of a loner you claim to be, at the end of the day, there is an unspoken need and desire to connect with other people. This desire is the foundation of human interaction. However, there are laws and rules that guide this process. These laws are not what you find in the constitution. What you should expect to find is the fact that there are socially acceptable behaviors that come to play when you are looking at human interaction. Beyond social skills and etiquette, this chapter was going to go in-depth on how this process works and you get some tips on playing this knowledge to your advantage.

The Basic Psychological Principles of Human Interaction

This segment is meant to focus on why we interact with each other as humans. By understanding the purpose of human interaction and the psychology that guides that process, we better equip ourselves with the right tools (or mindset if you prefer) that will get us to where we want socially.

The very first basic psychological principle of human interaction is the fact that every social relationship that we have serves a goal. Now, that goal may have been plotted out consciously and deliberately. Or sometimes, it is just something that we gravitate to naturally because it suits a need. In a situation where social interaction is deliberate, the person who makes a conscious effort to interact with specific people does it usually to meet a transactional need. For instance, the person may feel that by interacting with this particular individual, they may be able to get the opportunities that would lead to their growth in a work environment or their social status.

This is not to say that the person does it with malicious intent. This person simply sees social interaction as a means to an end. Now let us look at the flip side to this. On an unconscious level, you have this person who gravitates towards a person socially to meet some form of emotional need. This is very common with us, especially if we grew up lacking a parental figure or what we term as an ideal role model in our lives. We try to fill up that hole in our lives with the people that we meet and the relationships that we build with them. When we meet someone who we feel matches the profile of our expectations, we use the relationship that we have with them to replace our losses.

Going forward, it is important to understand why you are entering into relationships with people. And while you are on the subject, try to figure out why these people that you meet might be trying to establish relationships with you. Is it for emotional reasons or transactional reasons? The goal does not necessarily have to determine your acceptance of that relationship. It simply helps you understand where you stand with that person and how to proceed in terms of communication and all of the other topics we have addressed in the previous chapters.

Difference in Manipulation Vs Influence Based on True Connection, Intimacy and Serving Others

Given everything we have talked about so far, it is understandable if you start using the words, influence, and manipulations interchangeably. However, these words have two very distinct meanings and their application in relationships have the ability to break or build that relationship. It is therefore important to understand the differences between these two words. Because, if you take everything that you learn in this book and decide to use it to your advantage without really understanding the concept behind it, you would find that rather than building good and healthy relationships you have set the tone for manipulations and nobody likes to be manipulated.

Manipulations may yield you the results that you want temporarily, but it could go on to destroy whatever future that relationship had. Influence or the other hand, can impact the choices and decisions that the other person in the relationship with you makes. But, if you are coming from a place of genuine connection and intimacy, it has the ability to enhance communication and promote room for healthy growth. Manipulations involve the use of sinister and devious practices to get your way such practices could include lying, blackmail and threats masked as requests. Other forms of manipulations involve degrading a person to a point where they start to question their own opinions as well as the manipulation of elements in the environment to simulate control.

Influence, on the other hand, employs techniques such as concession, which is basically what happens during negotiation. It also uses authority so people in a position of authority can influence the people that they are leading. Another key principle of influence that a lot of us use is the simple act of 'likeness'. If you like a person, there is a very big possibility that you would go the extra mile for that person and a lot of us use this to our advantage. In this situation, the lines between manipulation and Influence might become blurred, but it tilts more towards influence because your emotions towards that person influence your decisions.

Jason Miller

Basic Ideas of What People Think in a Conversation and Social Interactions

If you have ever sat down during a conversation and thought to yourself, "what is this person thinking?", you are not alone. Beyond the subject matter of the conversation that we have with people, there is this innate curiosity that makes us wonder what our conversation mates are thinking. While it is impossible to decode those thoughts at the moment (given the fact that we have no mind reader), there are certain things that can clue us into the mindset of the person. I am not going to go into the specifics when it comes to the thoughts because, different strokes for different folks, as they say. However, I am going to go into some of the different things that can influence the thoughts of a person in social settings.

The Environment

The setting where you find yourself in plays a major role in what the person might be thinking about. For instance, if you are in a work environment, the line of thought would have to relate to the performance issues or anxieties about the performance issues. That is not to say that people in these environments do not think about anything outside the place of work. But this is in line with what is generally acceptable.

The Roles that They Play

The roles that people play influences what they think about in conversations or social interactions. For instance or parents would think more in the lines of things that affect the ability to parent as well as what impacts the future of their wards or children. So, if you find yourself in a conversation with a parent to enhance the conversation, you may want to find common ground by looking at their roles as parents. It is common knowledge that many parents are very proud of their children and the moment you strike up a conversation about their kids, it is always difficult to get them to stop (just kidding).

Their Emotional State

Around Valentine's season, cakes, cards, and flower vendors experience a spike in sales and when you look into their customer base, you find out that a lot of people who buy their products are couples or people who are intending to go into relationships. This speaks to the emotional state of people during that season. My point is, when striking up conversations with people, if you decode their emotional state accurately, you may be able to key into their thoughts and establish a connection with them. During Valentine, this is what these vendors tap into to make their sales pitch.

Jason Miller

Chapter Five

The Art of Small Talk

I think the biggest mistake a lot of people make is to assume that small talk is basically those pointless words that you use in an attempt to keep the conversation going. They failed to realize that small talk is the actual engine that drives a conversation. It may feel awkward initially, especially if you are not in an informal relationship with that person. However, if you do it right regardless of whatever phase that relationship is in, you can build a foundation that leads to death if it is what you desire. Whatever your relationship goals are, the fact remains that with small talk you can set the tone for the direction in the area of communication.

The Goal of Small Talk in Conversations

There are several reasons people use small talk in conversations and I will be going into some of them. However, just as I said in the introduction, small talk is a very important engine that is useful in driving a conversation. That said, let us look at the goals of small talk and perhaps, this will help you understand just how important it is.

1. It establishes a connection

Small talk typically evolves around relatable topics and with those kinds of topics, you can use it to get a feel of how the person you are communicating with sees the world without really getting in-depth. This is particularly useful if you are not familiar with the person in the first place. With small talk, you can get to know the person without making an awkward situation even more awkward.

2. It is a coping mechanism for people with anxiety

Social anxiety is more common than you think and we know that it happens when you find yourself in a social setting. If you are trying to break out of your shell and get into that place where communicating with people is no longer tedious, one of the first things you would have to learn how to do is small talk. Small talk is an excellent defense mechanism as it helps you participate in the conversation without dreading the outcome of it and this is because the conversation you are having is in shallow waters, so to speak and offers you safety.

3. It opens up a window for dialogue

This comes in very handy if you are at a networking event and you are trying to get to know people. Rather than coming outright and blurting out your credentials without really getting to know the person, inserting a little small talk into the conversation can set the premise for how the rest of your communication with that person will turn out. If you are able to do the small talk right, the person you are having a conversation with would be more open to hearing the rest of what you actually intend to say.

These three that I have just listed here are particularly useful for the objective that we have in terms of mastering the art of communication. The small talk goes beyond having to discuss the weather and in a few short moments, you are going to learn more on the subject. Just bear in mind that regardless of your personality type, small talk is essential for conversations to thrive.

Conversation Flow

If I wanted to give this topic a definition, I would say that conversation flow essentially is the smooth transition from one topic to another. When you are having an extensive conversation with a person, if you stay on one topic for too long, it might get boring. And if the topic is a sensational one, tempers might flare-up. So, it is important that you consciously apply effort in ensuring that the conversation moves freely from one topic to another. Now, in a bid to stir up the conversation flow, it is also important that you don't just jump from one topic to another. Because then, you start to look like you are unsure of what you are doing.

In this segment, I am going to guide you on how to establish a healthy conversation flow even with a stranger.

Step one: Create a doorway for the conversation

A doorway is the starting point for any conversation. Whether you are in an informal setting or any place where everyone is professional, you need a doorway to get you into a conversation. Now informal settings, a lot of people tend to go with the introduction route. They start a conversation by introducing themselves. That works too, but the most effective way to get the attention of a person you want to talk to in a formal setting is to bring the focus on them. What do I mean by that? Say you are aware of what the person does for a living, you can latch onto that as the introduction. An example of being, "Hi, I overheard that you are a software engineer. Do you work primarily with websites or applications?".

A question like that will force them to respond but there's also a great chance that they would respond happily because this is a subject that they are interested in. On the other hand, if you find yourself in an informal setting, a great way to stir up a conversation is by asking questions. However, ensure that the question you are asking is not a 'yes or no' kind of question. It should be a question that will cause them to be involved in their response. An example would be, "Hi there, I am very new at all this and you look like someone who is very much at home here. So, I was wondering if you could make a recommendation for me". Again this puts the person at the forefront of the conversation. If you ask politely and keep your demeanor pleasant, you might be able to start up a conversation.

The choice of the way for the conversation should be dependent on the situation you find yourself in. If you are on a date or an interview, or perhaps you are meeting up with investors, the doorway for the conversation must match the situation.

Step two: Initiate small talk

This is the part that some people have trouble with. But if you pay attention closely, I would say that this is the easiest part. The main ingredient for initiating good small talk is listening. Now, if you end up with a person who is not really into conversations, you may have to do more of the talking, but listen to their responses as well because their responses will cue you in on what the next topic of conversation should be. For example, if you meet the person in a museum and you were able to create a doorway for conversation, rather than ask them about when they developed their passion for art, focus on the little details that they offer you. For instance, if they mention the name of a particular artist, let that be a conversation lead. Make a comparison with the artist that they mentioned with another artist and get their opinions on it.

This is small talk, but in a way, it is helping you get to know the person. So, create the doorway then listen to their responses. Pick up on topics that you are knowledgeable about and find that they are also interested in to initiate the next topic of conversation. It is also fine if you allow the other person to lead you into the next topic. Avoid being monotonous in your responses. Giving yes or no answers when you are having a small talk is a big conversation killer. So, endeavor to respond in three to four sentences and perhaps ask a few questions of your own. As you ask your questions, try not to sound as though you are interrogating the person because that makes people defensive. Instead, affirm their choices and if you don't agree with them on certain topics, politely express your view without using it as an opportunity to convert them.

Step three: Time your conversation

If you keep the conversation short and sweet, people are more likely going to remember you. However, if you continue droning on about subjects that you find fascinating, there is a very big possibility that if that same person sees you at another event, they will avoid you. Especially if they don't share the same interests with you. So, when you get into conversations with people it is important that you time it in such a way that you are able to exit the conversation when the excitement is still high. There is a proverb that says, "leave when the applause is at its loudest." This applies to conversations as well. In a bid to keep your conversation short, I do not encourage you to be checking your time because of that in its own way as rude. However, there are body signs given by your partner in conversation that you can use to decide if it is time to exit that conversation.

For example, if you start noticing that the person you are talking to is glancing about the room, that is a sign that they are looking for someone else to talk to. At this point in time, this is your cue to step back. Another important cue to look out for is if they are checking their own time. These subtle body languages are informing you that the conversation has come to an end.

However, if you find that the conversation is riveting with both of you being reluctant to end it, I would still say that for a first meeting, especially if you are in a formal setting where the goal is networking, you should try to end the conversation. That said when you end the conversation with someone like this, ensure that you take their contact details as this could lead to more conversations or communications in the future. But as of the moment, your focus in this setting is to network and you want to mingle and meet up with as many people as possible.

If you are going to stick to time, then I will say in a formal setting, 5 minutes is a lot to spend with one person. That should not mean you end the conversation abruptly. You listen to what they have to say, express your fascination with their ideas and then inform them that you were pleased to meet them; however, it is time for you to move on. Exchange cards where possible and exit the conversation politely.

5 Principles For Success In Conversations

Given everything we have learned so far from the art of small talk to ensure that you have a smooth and healthy conversation flow, this segment is going to break down the guiding principles of a successful conversation. This will go on to help you identify those elements that make the conversation interesting, relatable and most importantly guarantees a repeat;

1. You are good with descriptions

In the mouth of a good conversationalist, words are like the paintbrush in the hand of a painter. The words that you use help to paint a mental picture and that picture is what your conversation partner would identify with. Your inability to use words to describe or articulate your thoughts is the reason why people have miscommunications. Because the words paint a different picture from the message that is being passed across. This is something that you are going to have to learn and groom yourself in.

2. Creative use of contrasts and comparisons

When having conversations, the comparisons and contrasts that you use have a way of enriching the image that you create. For example, instead of just saying that the beauty (of a person or thing you are describing) is delicate, you go on to say the beauty of that person is as delicate as a rose flower. What you have done there is to make the picture you are painting richer and all the more interesting. Comparisons that you use enhances the richness of a conversation.

3. The use of body language

The use of body language in a conversation is essential for the success of that conversation. Whether you like it or not, subconsciously, you are sending out messages with your body. Now, if you make a deliberate effort to ensure that the gestures you make and the facial expressions that you have matches the tempo of your conversation, you sound more interesting. And the reason for that is, your body language animates the conversation.

4. Voice inflection

Excitement can be infectious and the reason for this has been linked to the way we express our excitement. Apart from our non-verbal communication, which includes body language and facial expression, there is also our voice inflection. Have you noticed that when you are excited, your voice pitch takes on a different note? The ability to control your voice inflection is the reason why a lot of radio personalities able to drive interesting conversations over the radio even though you are not actively involved in that communication. When your voice pitch takes on a single monotonous pattern, you become bored quickly. That kind of speech pattern is best reserved for bedtime routines for children as it has the ability to induce sleep. During conversations, you want to keep it interesting so, learn to fluctuate in your voice pitch. Just remember that when you go too high, you sound crazy and when you get too low, you sound weird. Keep your pitch range somewhere in the middle.

5. Interesting topics

When you are having conversations with people, the topic focus should not just be a subject that you find interesting. Your partner in the conversation has to find that topic interesting too. That way, both your interests intersect. You may be one of those people who can talk about the incubation period of the caterpillar and find it so fascinating. However, not everybody is interested in the sordid details surrounding this phenomenon. So, as I mentioned in the previous segment, pick up cues as to what both of you find interesting and elaborate on that. If you apply all of the four previously mentioned principles of a successful conversation, it is bound to make the topic even more engaging.

Having laid out these five basic principles, I feel like I should point out here that no conversation can truly become successful if you fail to listen to your conversation partner. The cues for your conversation guide will come from the details obtained when you listen to that person. You may enjoy the sound of your voice and you may have some interesting contributions to make to that conversation; however, you must remember that conversation is not entirely about you and therefore, you need to give room for the other person to share their thoughts and opinions.

Chapter Six

How to Initiate Non-Verbal Communication

Before you open your mouth to speak, there are ways that your body can communicate. The information that you put out there with your body even though it is subconscious could go a long way in helping other people around you form an opinion about you. For instance, if you are in a public space and you are standing with your arms crossed across your chest, people immediately get the way that you do not want to have a conversation. And even though this is not your intention, your body language is saying you are a no-go area. So, this chapter is about helping you learn how to be more deliberate in the way you communicate without saying a word.

How to Smile

A smile is an involuntary response to something that makes you happy or brings you joy. There are a lot of scientific studies that have been conducted on the benefits of a smile and the results of these studies have linked smiles with longevity, health as well as attractiveness. It is said that smiling makes you more physically attractive and not just to yourself but to the people around you. Now, this attraction is not just about physical beauty. What this means here is that a smile can act as a social magnet that attracts people to you. When you smile in a public space, essentially, you are speaking non-verbally and telling the people around you that you are approachable and available for a conversation.

I did say that as well as an involuntary response; however, it doesn't mean that you can only smile when you feel happy or see something that gives you joy. You can deliberately initiate a smile even though you are not experiencing any of these emotions I mentioned. When I was younger, my mother was very fond of saying this, "fake it until you make it," and she was talking about my smile. I wasn't much of the smiler and anytime we went out, she was constantly encouraging me to smile. At first, when I curve my lips upwards in an attempt to smile, I felt ridiculous and somewhat embarrassed. But I found that as the seconds progressed, I genuinely started feeling like I needed to smile. Going by my experience, of course, in that first stage, the smile can seem painful. If you have ever witnessed a painful smile, you know what I mean... that one where your teeth are grinding against each other and the muscles on the side of your face become strained from the effort you are putting into a smile. That, in my opinion, is not a smile. It is a grimace.

The key to faking a smile is keeping it as natural as possible. And since we already know that a smile is an involuntary reaction to something that gives you joy, we start by focusing on elements around you that make you happy. It could be the color used in the decoration; it could be the snacks that were served, or you could focus on people that you actually like. If the atmosphere around you does not appeal to you in any way, then you could focus internally. Draw on images that make you smile; it could be an old joke or the thought of engaging in an activity that you enjoy. Let these pleasant memories motivate your smile. Now when you do smile, try not to display all of your dentition at once because then you look ridiculous and scary. A small but genuine smile is all it takes to get the wagon rolling.

How to use your eyes/body language

In romantic folklore, they say that the eyes are the windows to the soul. I don't know how true that is, but I do know this; if you do not channel your gaze properly, you can come across as one of many things and one of those things could be the vibe that you are an unpleasant person to be around. When you step into a new environment and you find yourself glancing around, people read you as someone who is nervous and with something to hide. If you decide to glare at people every time they look at you, the interpretation they will get is that you are a person with malicious intent. This also happens when it comes to body language. If your arms or legs are crossed, whether you are standing or sitting, it reads as though you are turning people away. The message that they get from you, essentially, is that you are not available for conversation.

Even if you are not having a one-on-one conversation with people, if you find yourself in a position where you are on a stage talking to a crowd of people, your body language can either support the words you are saying or contradict them. You can use your eyes to express interest in a person or express your disgust of their person. Your eyes can also make a person feel intimidated by your presence, or you can help that person feel as though they are welcome into your space. The language of the eyes and the body is one of the most basic forms of communication. When you

Jason Miller

were born, you did not have the gift of garb, yet somehow, your parents can read your expression and understand that you have certain feelings about certain things... even though you never expressly stated those emotions. As we grow into languages and understand how to communicate without words, our eyes and our bodies still have an essential message to pass across.

More often than not, I believe that our bodies have a way of communicating the true intent of our hearts. Even if your words are saying one thing, people are paying attention to the way your hands are moving and to the expressions on your face. I remember a hilarious incident that happened when I was much younger. My younger sister was being introduced to lime. We talked about the lime; about how sharp and bitter, the taste was. But this particular brother of mine was bragging about how he loved the taste of lime and so, my mother bought lime for him that day. He tasted it and of course, immediately, he was hit with the sharp sensations and although the words that came out from his mouth were, "I love it," we saw his facial expression and it told us everything we needed to know. His eyes were squeezed shot which basically told us that he could not stand the taste and his face was scrunched up in a way that further emphasized what the eyes were already telling us.

Our body language and our expressions during conversation may not be as intense as my brother's lime lying experiment, however, for people who pay attention to your body language, they get the true message just as clearly as we did.

Jason Miller

How to Come Across and Credible and Confident Without Words

Even for the most social person, I would say that it is not every time they walk into a room full of people that they immediately feel confident. They are simply just better adept at masking their emotions. In this segment, we are going to focus on those non-verbal ways to communicate your confidence even before you say a single word. There are several books that focus on this subject because of the volume of information available on this. However, I am going to keep it short and simple by focusing on the basics. As you continue to practice your conversation skills, you would evolve and grow this list.

1. Dress the part

The dressing has a way of building your confidence, and when you look confident, you feel confident. If you are invited to an event, endeavor to put work towards ensuring that the clothes you wear to the event match the theme. That way, you do not stand out as the oddball. One thing I would like you to take note of here is that dressing the part does not mean you have to spend a lot of money on your clothing or wear designer gear. There are three things you need to focus on when it comes to dressing the part. One is your comfort, two is your style and then three is the fit of the outfit.

Comfort does not necessarily mean you have to wear slacks and bunny slippers. Comfort is ensuring that you are able to move around comfortably in that outfit without feeling as though your dressing is going to fall apart. It also means prioritizing what makes you feel comfortable over what is fashionable. So, a nice pair of flats may be more comfortable for you than a six-inch heel. The heels are very attractive and fashionable, but you risk falling down and injuring yourself. It is better to stick with sensible shoes. Choose a pair that are formal. The next part is your style. If you are not into high fashion drama, there is no need to get into the latest trends. Stick to what you genuinely enjoy. When it comes to style, again, all you need to keep in mind is ensuring that your personal style is in tandem with the theme for the event you are attending.

Finally, ensure that the clothes you are wearing are fitted. When clothes match your body size perfectly, it enhances your strengths and hides your flaws, making you look exceptionally beautiful or handsome, as the case may be. This goes on to provide you with confidence.

2. Maintain a good posture

Slouched shoulders, hunched back and a low-hanging chin are classic indicators of poor confidence and low self-esteem issues. So it is important that you maintain a good posture. Stand upright, keep your head held up high and avoid slouching your shoulders. The key to attaining the perfect posture is just like attaining a natural smile. You have to try to keep your posture as natural as possible so that you don't come off looking stiff. Because, if you look stiff, the message you are passing across to people who might be coming your way is that you are someone who is not fun and we both know that you are an amazing person for people to know. All you have to do is give them a chance. It starts by keeping the doors open. What do I mean? Ensure that your posture says you are welcoming, inviting and accessible.

Jason Miller

3. Don't run away from direct contact

When you meet someone, you instinctively reach out your hand for a handshake. This is a ritual in communication that must be adhered to. When you are in a handshake, ensure that your grip is firm. However, don't make it too firm that you hurt the person. Another thing you have to try to do is to maintain eye contact. Averting your gaze when there is a contact might be interpreted as you being either shy or lacking when it comes to confidence. A confident person is able to hold another person's gaze. If you feel that it is too tedious to maintain eye contact with a person, try this simple trick I learned. Gaze at the person for 10 seconds, then look away to a distance that is no longer than 10 feet away from you for another 10 seconds before returning your gaze to the person. This way, you don't have to feel intimidated by that process.

You engage the person with your eyes, take your gaze away for a few seconds and then return the focus to that person. In a more intimate setting, I would advise that you hold that gaze for longer. It builds the connection you have with that person.

Chapter Seven

Becoming a Master at Small Talk

Small talk is the engine that drives a conversation which eventually leads to building lasting relationships. If you are able to master the art of small talk, you will become an excellent conversationalist. People love to talk with someone who has something interesting to say. But more importantly, they also want to be heard. Small talk is not just about you talking.

It is about creating an atmosphere that allows for easy communication and communication can only happen if you allow the other person to have room to express their opinions. And just so you know, the subject of the small talk does not really matter as long as you are able to handle it delicately.

You could be discussing the weather and still make it such a fascinating subject that the other person involved becomes engaged. This is what it means to master small talk.

How to Start Small Talk

Knowing what we know now about small talk, here are a few pointers to help you get started;

Step one: Put your phone aside

Small talk is not the time to start showing off the make and model of your phone or trying to view the latest happening on Instagram. Social media has made it possible for us to connect with people all over the world; however, because of the numerous voices on the platform, it has made us more disconnected from our real world. I watched a movie once where this nice family was having dinner. And the whole room was quiet, not because the food was super delicious, but because everyone was on their phone. A platform where the family was supposed to connect with each other gave room for a total disconnect because of phones. So it is important that you disconnect from social media and your phone in order to connect with the person in front of you.

Step two: Ask open-ended questions

I talked about this earlier, but I didn't go into detail because I knew that we were going to run into this here. The questions that you ask will elicit a response from the person that you are talking to. If you ask simple 'yes or no' type of questions, that is exactly what you would get. You need to learn to ask the type of questions that would require the person responding to use more than two sentences.

Step three: Be enthusiastic

Remember what I said about voice inflections earlier. When you inject excitement into your words, it automatically triggers excitement in the other person. This is because, as humans, we are empathetic by nature and one of the ways we show empathy is by mirroring the action or response of the other person in conversation. Your enthusiasm can become contagious simply because the person empathizes with where you are coming from and they are now mirroring your reaction. It may feel a little fake initially, but the more you practice, the better you become at being excited about the topic of your small talk

Step four: Listen attentively

One thing I have always said in this book is that the foundation for your small talk is basically in the answers that you receive. When you ask those open-ended questions, the responses that you get are what will build the topic for the next set of questions and that is essentially how your conversation will grow. So, pay attention. Besides, you never can tell when the other person would ask a question of their own and if you weren't paying attention or listening to anything they were saying, you might end up making yourself and the person look like a fool.

Step five: Choose your small talk topics carefully

Small talk is not a time to express your political and religious views. Not only is there a very strong possibility that you might end up offending the person you are having a conversation with, but it also creates room for animosity and can make the person that you are having this conversation with feel defensive. When people are defensive, their guards are thrown up, leaving you on the outside. Safe topics for conversation include arts, sports, hobbies, professional interests and of course, my personal favorite, climate.

Jason Miller

How To use the FORD Method For Small Talk

The last segment rounded off with the instruction to be careful about the choice of topics for your small talk. There I listed a few examples; however, the Ford method is one of the most reliable ways to decide on the preferred topic for small talk, especially if you are having a conversation with a complete stranger. The Ford method essentially focuses on the acronym FORD, and it means;

F = Family
O = Occupation
R = Recreation
D = Dreams

These are the safest topics to go for when initiating small talk with new people. One thing you should bear in mind, though, is the fact that people react differently to certain questions. This is because they all have their own personal experiences and those experiences are not always pleasant. For instance, a person who is not in very good standing with their family may not be too excited about talking on that subject. It is now left for you to take cues from what they say as well as their body language. The second you get that standoffish or defensive vibe from them, that is your cue to drop the subject. Do not proceed if you sense that the person you are trying to have a conversation with is not comfortable with the choice of topic. That will only ruin things for you and them.

How to Ask Excellent Questions

You would not believe the amount of diplomacy that is required in sustaining a healthy conversation even if you are just meeting that person for the first time. The reason for this diplomacy is that we live in a very sensitive world and people are now beginning to discover and leave their personal truths. Your opinions no longer govern the lives of other people. Now, I am not saying that it did back in the day. It's just that people were more tolerant of outside opinions. Not to mention the fact that they were very into ensuring that their lives were pleasing to those around them.

But all of that is rapidly changing and for this reason, you have to apply caution when you ask certain questions. Even if you are genuinely curious about what is going on in that person's life and you are certain that you have no ulterior motive, you need to respect the boundaries that people have put up and unless you are invited, certain doors on certain subjects will always remain shut. This segment is about helping you find a way to ask those open-ended questions that will not offend or cause the person you are asking those questions to feel insulted. See what I mean about being diplomatic? Anyways, let us get into it.

As I mentioned earlier and open-ended question is basically the kind of question that would require the person in the conversation that has been asked to respond in more than one sentence because it would require them to use their own knowledge and feelings an example of an open-ended question is, " what have you been up to today?". You see that there is no way a person can answer yes or no to that question, they would have to break down how their day went even if they may prefer to give the paraphrased version.

Typically, open-ended questions begin with any of the following words; why, what, describe and explain. The last two words on the list are not really questionnaires on their own; however, they can be used to elicit a lengthy response from the person you are conversing with. If your questions begin with a will, do, are, and so on, the response you are going to get is going to either be a yes or a no with little to no explanation.

The Power of Listening

There are several definitions of the word, listening. However, I would say that the one that most appeals to me is this one that says, "listening is the mindful act of hearing and making an attempt to comprehend what is being said by the other person." In other words, listening is not just hearing the words that being said to you. It is a choice that you have to make to understand what is being said to you. These days a lot of people feel that communication means talking and because we all have something to say, we feel that it must be said. And in our bid to ensure that what we have to say comes out, we fail to pay attention to the words that are coming out from the mouths of the people around us.

Active listening I am told is an essential communication skill. You cannot call yourself a great conversationalist if you fail in the area of listening. What that says about your person is that you are only concerned about your voice as well as the voice in your head. Every other person's opinion might as well be dust; you receive it, but you never make use of it. No matter how smooth you are when it comes to the gift of garb, if you are not a listener, you will not be able to engage your audience. Even in shows where you have comedians on stage doing their bit, despite the fact that the only person doing the talking is the comedian, he or she still listens to the audience for cues and it is those cues that help him deliver his performance exquisitely well.

We have already established that there is both verbal and nonverbal communication. For conversations to go smoothly, you have to pay attention to both what is being said and the body language you are getting from the person. In a situation where you have multiple people talking at once, there is very little possibility of the cause of the problem being resolved and that's because everyone is talking at the same time. The solution will only arise when one person decides to listen and hear the other party out.

Mastering the art of small talk and knowing when to listen are two of the basic skills you need in order to become an excellent conversationalist.

Chapter Eight

Channeling Positivity into Your Conversation to Keep it Going

Before we go any further into this chapter, I want to say congratulations. You have come a long way from where we started and while we still have some ways to go, it is important to sit back and take note of the progress you have made so far. I also hope that at the end of each chapter, you give yourself social assignments to carry out so that you can experiment on the lessons you have learned. This is not the kind of book that you open and read from chapter to chapter, back to back, until the end.

I think that would be boring and at the same time, it will not help you assimilate the information that I have compressed into this book. So, in case you haven't been doing this already, at the end of each chapter (if possible at the end of each segment), close the book and carry out a physical social experiment. Create journals to record your experiences and proffer solutions with a focus on how you think you can improve in those areas you feel you fell short on. Now that we are done with that, let's get right on to the gist of this chapter.

How to Talk and Banter

On the surface level, talk and banter have the same meaning. However, when you go deeper into the definition of things, especially when it comes to conversations, there is a lot of difference. Talk is all we have been doing since we started this journey together from the first chapter.

We have been looking at how to talk better, how to engage in small talk and generally just how to be better at talking with people. Banter, on the other hand, is a playful type of conversation. This is the kind of conversation you have with a person whom you are typically attracted to. Sometimes, we have playful conversations with people who are just friends, family members or even people of the same sex. However, for this segment, we are focusing on playful banter with the opposite sex because yes, that is part of communication too.

One major rule of banter conversation is ensuring that both you and the person (s) engaged in the conversation are aware of the fact that everything said in that conversation cannot be taken seriously. You need to apply the law of taking things with the proverbial pinch of salt because everything that you say in that conversation should not be given any kind of levity. The main ingredient for a successful banter conversation is a great sense of humor as well as this mutual understanding that I just talked about. You should be able to roll with the punches and dish out just as much as you are receiving. I have heard of banter conversations that took on a nasty turn and then again, that is not why we are here. We are looking at how to keep the conversation playful and sexy when dealing with the opposite sex without turning ourselves into maniacs.

Another important thing to remember is that banter is a playful exchange and the goal is to tease each other. This is where you display your wit. And as far as I am concerned, there is nothing sexier than wit and humor. In the spirit of keeping things playful and light, your body language should also reflect this. That stern and stiff body posture are not going to work. You need to loosen up a little. That is not to say that you should hunch your back and drop your chin. We talked about this earlier. You have to look confident. But in this case, you also have to look relaxed. Looking stiff and holding your breath at the same time will make you look constipated and I have never known anyone to like that. Finally, you have to learn to have fun with this. You are not writing an exam that your life depends on. You are simply bantering. Also, the only way to become good at bantering is practice. The more you engage in it, the faster you develop the ability to think on your feet.

How to Always have something interesting to Say

Chances are, you have met that one person who is just such a delight to talk to. They always have something to say that stirs up the conversation. That person is what we call a great conversationalist. The thing is, a great conversationalist is not someone who always has something to say. It goes beyond that. After all, is said and done, the best thing about a great conversationalist is the fact that they enter into conversations without any expectations. They don't even try to control the conversation; they just go with the flow. The only time you would find them actively guiding the conversation is when they feel that the topic is veering off into murky waters. Other than that, they just go with it. No matter what is being discussed, they seem to have an idea about it and have the ability to make a valuable contribution to that conversation. This could also be you and here's how to ensure that you always have something interesting to say;

1. Stay up to date on all current events

If you were thinking that the 10 o'clock news was for older people, I am hoping that after this segment, you will change that mindset. The local news basically, is information about what is going on in the world around us. You cannot be so consumed with your life that you fail to be aware of what this is going on. Your awareness of the latest happenings will form a major part of the contribution that you make in any conversation. A great conversationalist always stays updated.

2. Read a book

This book you have in your hand right now will provide a wealth of information that goes beyond just what you were hoping you will get from it when you opened the first page. This is what all books are like. They open you up to a world that you are not familiar with. They transport you to places and times. You can go back in time to visit the past or take a trip to the future. There is just so much information available in a book. Since information is essential for a good conversation, you may need to develop the habit of reading.

3. Think carefully about your answers before you respond

Unlike playful banter, where you allow the first thing that pops into your head to come out of your mouth, this time around you need to think carefully before you respond. At the same time, do not try to force yourself to sound interesting. People can see through your attempts and they would see as someone who is not genuine. In a bid to make yourself sound interesting, you might end up losing the interest of the person you are having a conversation with. Be relaxed, think your answers through and respond in a way that is respectful and befitting of the question you are trying to answer or contribution you are trying to make to that conversation.

How to Resuscitate a Dying Conversation

There are times when no matter how much effort you put into a conversation, we find that things are slowly drifting into a deep end. It is like watching a drunk man trying to walk on a straight line. He has very little control over his limbs and constantly teeters over an imaginary edge. In the same way, you are feeling powerless to stop the death of the conversation. I have been in that situation so many times that I can read the signs of the back of my palm. The banter slowly dies and then people start fidgeting and avoiding each other's gaze. Occasionally, you will hear someone cough here and there. When you see all these signs, know that that conversation is dying. However, it doesn't have to. By injecting your personality into the conversation and taking control of the wheel without necessarily trying to control what people say, you can get the conversation back on track. Here are my tips to help you do so without losing a single drop of sweat

Jason Miller

Step one: Don't take it too personally

A lot of times, we assume responsibility for a dying conversation. We feel that it is because we don't have anything to contribute, or we have just too shy to say anything of value that people will find interesting. But this is not the case. Sometimes, people are genuinely tired and when they are tired, a conversation is the last thing on their mind. You have to respect that and don't try to carry the weight of the conversation. If you get the sense that people are tired, let it go. There will always be other times to chat. This is the one time you should accept that it is not your fault. It takes two to dialogue. As long as you tried to put in some effort and you are not getting feedback, you are good.

Step two: Put your newly developed small talk skill to work

If you have been practicing how to engage people with small talk, this is the best time to put it to work. Perhaps the weight of the previous conversation is making people feel uncomfortable. Small talk eases them out of that discomfort and can get the conversation going again. Remember, we talked about the FORD method. This will also be a good place to apply it

Step three: Ask questions and listen attentively to the response

Remember we talked about asking open-ended questions. This is also a great place to put that to work. The questions that we ask will give you more insight into the person and also give them the opportunity to talk (that is if they are interested in talking). I know that previously, I also emphasized the fact that it is the information that you get during this exchange, that will build on the next question. And this is just how you keep going and growing that conversation

Step four: Know when to call it a day

Here's the thing; at some point, you are going to have just to accept that perhaps this person or persons are not interested in having a conversation. And that is okay. It does not reflect directly on your person. We just talked about this in step one; this has to do with the other person. You can't control how they feel about the conversation or their decision to not contribute to the conversation. This is on them and if you are getting this kind of vibe, I would say it is best to check out politely.

How to Come Across as a Positive Person

People naturally gravitate towards someone that they perceive has warm and positive energy. Nobody wants to stand or talk with the bitter crow. And whether you like it or not, there are subconscious vibes that you give off that tells the state of your mind. The subconscious vibe I am talking about here goes beyond your body language. A positive person has a cheery disposition. I would like to point out here that being shy has very little to do with your disposition. I mention this because a lot of people tend to confuse the aversion that shy people have towards social settings with the aversion that a negative person has towards people.

Even if you are shy, it doesn't mean that you are automatically a negative person. A shy person essentially has trouble connecting with people in a social setting and a negative person on the other hand, also experiences trouble connecting people in social settings. But their experiences are not because of the same reasons.

For a negative person, it has more to do with the character traits and dark personality, which makes people avoid them. People don't avoid a shy person, as a matter of fact, because of the quiet nature of the shy person, a lot of people are not even aware of the shy person's presence. But I can tell you that they see a negative person clearly and make a choice to avoid them completely.

To project yourself as a positive person, you would have to do the opposite of everything that the negative person does

1. Do not look down condescendingly on other people

Negative people have a very condescending manner about them. It is almost as if they feel that everyone that they come in contact with is meant to serve them. A positive person, on the other hand, looks at everyone they meet as equals. It doesn't matter your gender, appearance or social status; a positive person automatically finds a way to connect with you. On the other hand, a negative person is looking for reasons to disconnect from you.

2. Do not talk people down when you meet them

This is a classic negative person move. It is all part of the condescending strategy. Sometimes, their talking down on people is not necessarily because they are very mean. They use it to mask their own insecurities. So, if they find that a person is making a more valuable contribution to a conversation than they are, their strategy is to find a way to break that person's confidence. And they do this by talking down on them. A negative person does not appreciate the confidence in a person; instead, they see it as a threat or a challenge. A positive person, on the other hand, is constantly seeking to cheer you on. So, even when people falter in conversations, a positive person does not take that as a limitation or nuisance; instead, they encourage the person.

3. Do not engage any negative thoughts

If you are in a social setting, it is possible that the ambiance may not be as beautiful or as up to standard as you would like it to be. And these things could be in your head as you are ruminating on the entire situation. However, a positive person does their best to ensure that what is in their head, stays in their head. As a matter of fact, they go a step further by focusing on the details that are actually nice. That way, the thoughts invoke pleasant feelings and these pleasant feelings radiate into the aura. A negative person, on the other hand, takes delight in tearing apart the efforts of other people. And so they have no trouble thinking negative things and then even going a step further to air out their negative views regardless of who they hurt along the way.

Avoiding Excessive Negativity in Your Social Interactions

Now that you have figured out how to project yourself as a positive person, it is time to look at a scenario where you have other people projecting negativity on you.

Just because you are trying to maintain a dialogue and build a relationship doesn't mean that you should have to take on their negativity as well. If you have learned anything along the way, I hope it includes the fact that emotions are contagious. Just as people can contact excitement from your own excitement, you can also catch negative emotions from the negativity of other people. Besides avoiding the concept or the idea of being around negative people, there is also the fact that negativity is an energy-draining exercise. If you have ever been near a with a negative person, you know exactly what I am talking about.

You spend resources, energy and effort trying to fight off that negative spirit and by the time you are done with them, you would feel exhausted. And the worst part is that you wouldn't have made any positive progress. So, resist the urge to be the person who changes the negativity of other people. If you find that you are already feeling emotionally drained every time you encounter a particular person, you need to start looking out for your own mental health. Now, stepping out of that situation takes courage. Especially if you are a shy person who is just learning how to connect with people. If you find out this person you have connected with has such negative energy, it is heartbreaking for starters. Secondly, it is difficult to get out of that situation because you know how much you struggled to even get into the relationship in the first place. But that is what the segment is about.

Before we get into how to avoid negative energy, let us talk about the signs that tell you, you are in a negative environment

1. Someone is getting hurt

In relationships, there will be times where we unintentionally hurt the other person. This kind of hurt is never deliberate and the moment it is brought to the attention of the person who is inflicting that hurt, immediately they feel remorseful and take steps to resolve the situation. However, in a negative environment, the goal is to hurt. Whether you are the one being hurt or you and the person you are with are collaborating to hurt other people, that is a negative situation and you need to get out of it.

2. You feel as though you are constantly fighting a battle

Relationships are never easy and that is because you have to diplomatically navigate through your needs, wants and compromises. However, if it feels as though everything in that relationship is an uphill climb, you may want to rethink that situation. Relationships are not really as hard as people say they are. Yes, you will encounter challenges the same when you encounter challenges in life, but if you are constantly fighting and feeling emotionally drained at the end of the day, you need to get out.

3. You have no sense of self-worth

Positive relationships have a way of reinforcing your strengths and helping you work on your weaknesses. If you are in a relationship or a situation where you feel that your weaknesses are constantly on display and your confidence is taking a beating on a daily basis, that relationship is very negative. It lacks the nurturing and encouragement that is abundant in positive relationships.

There are many more signs to look out for but these three are classic. So, I urge you to pay attention to. If you find yourself in that situation, it may be hard at first but you need to look out for yourself and take that bold step to get out of that situation. Now, if you are in a networking event or a social setting that has a semblance of a networking event, there is a chance that you would find negative people. Because where you have people in a gathering, you would find clusters of negative energy around the place. You need to step out of those clusters to avoid negative conversations.

This is how to recognize this kind of situation and avoid them:

1. When people are engaging in gossip or hurtful rumors, it may sound delightful to the ears. But remember, someone is getting hurt in that conversation. Even if the person being talked about is not

present, you need to get yourself out of that group.

2. When a group of people seems to have nothing positive to say about the event, you can interject and let them know that you see some positive things. If they ignore the things you have highlighted and still go on to talk about their negative perspective, you should take that as your cue to leave that conversation.

3. If you find yourself in a cluster where the body language is dark and unwelcoming, this is a sign that the atmosphere there is negative. You don't even need to wait for a conversation, quietly pick up your things and move to somewhere where the ambiance is more receptive.

Chapter Nine

Using the Art of Storytelling to Drive Conversations

One of my favorite things about my childhood was the bedtime stories that my parents would read to me before I go to bed. More often than not, they prefer to go outside the books that they bought for me because I was the kind of child who got bored with monotony. So, they had to learn how to tell stories that I had never heard before and I tell you, it was the best thing ever. I think that it was because of those bedtime stories that I learned how to be a good storyteller. Even though I was very shy, for the people that I knew and connected with daily, they enjoyed it when I was telling a story.

It could be something as simple as my experience at the office. I learned how to add little embellishments and use certain words to make my story billboard worthy. In this chapter, I am going to draw from my own experiences as well as the opinions of experts to help you perfect the art of telling a good story. This will go on to help you perfect the art of keeping your conversation partners engaged. It is the art of storytelling that makes it possible for a great conversationalist to talk about the weather as though he or she were reading a transcript from one of Sidney Sheldon's novels.

Principles of a Good Storyteller

For starters, a good story is about an event and how the people in that story reacted to that event. A great storyteller has a good story to tell and so for you to become a great storyteller, you have to start with your story. So, let us explore the elements of a good story

1. It comes from an experience

The one thing you should know is that experiences don't have to be something that you went through first-hand. It could be something that you experience through another person. Perhaps it was a story that they shared with you or it was something that you witnessed. Either way, for a story to be good, you need to involve experience. The reason is that when you experience something, you are able to explore that experience with your senses; you know what you felt, or heard or even smelled

2. It should have a series of unexpected events

The twist and turns in the story are what makes it engaging and riveting to the listener. If your story is something that people have heard consistently, over time, they may get bored or not feel half as connected to the story as they would if everything you are laying out with something that was unexpected.

3. It can be embellished but not fabricated

Even the greatest storytellers and fictional writers draw on the experiences of other people to tell their stories. What they write about is not entirely fabricated. There are elements of truth in their stories. What they do however is to embellish the details and make it as unexpected as possible. For an introverted person, this stage here is going to be a very

Jason Miller

tough hill to climb. However, with some practice, you will get the hang of it.

How to Keep the Other Person Engaged and Listening

In the last segment, our focus was on the elements of a good story. In this segment, we are going to look at how to tell that story. Now, these are two different things but if you are able to bring them together in harmony, you would greatly improve your storytelling skills. So, let us begin

1. Speak in the language that they understand

Storytelling is lost on your listener if they are unable to comprehend you or the things you are saying. Language here goes beyond the commonly accepted native tongue. It is also about vocabulary. If you are talking with children, you would have to bring yourself down to their level and this would also include using words that they can understand. You cannot bring the University standard language into a preschool class and expect that they would understand what you are saying. In the same way, gauge the audience you are with and measure they are receptiveness to your language and then tone it down or up as the case may be, to suit their level of comprehension.

2. Tell your story from a relatable context

If people can't relate to the story that you are telling, there is a very strong possibility that you would lose them. Your message may be a very powerful and life-changing one but if they cannot understand how it impacts them or where they feature in it, you might lose your audience. One way to make your story relatable is to personalize it. Don't approach it with a futuristic perspective or out of body experience. Bring it down to a level where they feel as though they were a part of that story. Emphasize your personal experiences in that story. Highlight what you felt and how you felt and then tie that into the theme of the present conversation you are having.

3. Be animated in the delivery of your story

We talked about voice pitches and voice inflections earlier on and this goes on to emphasize that. When telling a story, if you use the same monotonous tone and expressionless face in your description, you will lose your audience before you get to the end of that story. Try as much as possible to be animated. Let your voice inject as much emotion as possible into the story. Think of it as a stage performance except that you are not on stage and your audience is not paying for your performance. However, the routine is the same. The main actor here is your voice and if you use your voice inflections correctly, you could create different characters in your story and the audience will connect with each of them.

All of this is something that you would have to learn and practice. Some experts recommend taking Improv classes to improve your storytelling skills. I say that is an excellent idea. Go for it if you can.

Chapter Ten

Building Quality Relationships and the Keys to Making Them Last

There is an old African adage that says, "when the handshake extends beyond the elbows, it becomes something else." From the first chapter to the 9th chapter of this book, our focus was establishing the foundation for relationships that first communication you have with people that then goes on to build lasting relationships. Now, we have gone past that proverbial handshake. We are now trying to get to the elbow. This is a different ball game altogether. You would need to learn new skills and this is apart from the ones that you are already developing. Some of it will come naturally to you and some of it will take some patience and understanding to get through it. This chapter is about walking you through that process. I intend to help you build good and healthy relationships no matter how much of an introvert you are.

Connecting with People by Finding Common Ground

Human beings are communal creatures. We are biologically programmed to find and connect with people who we have something in common with. The key to lasting relationships is ensuring that you are connecting with people that you can relate with. If you have nothing in common with this person whatsoever, it can be very difficult for that relationship to thrive. And the reason for this is because at some point it would seem as though the relationship is one-sided. When a relationship becomes one-sided, it becomes a breeding ground for resentment.

Today, the world has experienced the highest rate of divorce than it ever has in recent years. And if you look closely at the people involved and have a conversation with them, you would find that the whole relationship crumbled because of resentment. I have listened to interviews of people who were getting divorced or trying to salvage a damaged relationship, one of the recurrent themes in those conversations was the fact that they felt like they no longer had anything in common with this person. It is very important to have common grounds in a relationship and so before you even get into it, you have to ensure that both parties have something in common.

It could be a business goal if you are talking about formal relationships. Or shared values and belief systems if you are talking about informal relationships. Do not connect with people based on trivial things like their appearance or wealth. Over time, those things will fade away. The important things to look for are their character traits, their personalities, their dreams, and their ambitions. These are things that remain consistent over time. And when you get to know these things, you have to be able to see where you fit in because your fitting into their world as well as their fitting into your world establishes common ground. That way both worlds can come together without colliding. Lasting relationships are built through the merging of worlds and it starts from finding common ground.

How to Make Them Feel You Empathize

In today's world, the concept of empathy has evolved from its original meaning. Without going through the whole psychological babble, let me just put it this way; empathy is basically walking in the other person's shoes. In other words, you put yourself in that person's situation and have a second-hand experience of what they are going through. Today, a lot of people feel that empathy is about saying nice things when people are going through stuff. That is not empathy. That is being kind and showing compassion. Empathy allows you to understand a person's point of view and like I said, for you to be able to do that, you would have to walk in their shoes. In this case, it doesn't have to mean you going through exactly what they are going through. You would have to put your imagination to work. Picture the circumstances that they are going through, insert yourself in that situation and then look at things from that perspective. This will give you a unique understanding of a person's behavior, thoughts, and motives.

In relationships, we tend to focus on our needs and this is because we fail to empathize with those of our partners. When someone reacts to you or something that you did, we take it personally because we feel that it is more about us than them. While I am a strong advocate for making yourself the number one lead character in your life, I feel that if you want your relationship to thrive, you may have to get off your soapbox from time to time and view things from the other person's perspective. When you have the perspective of the other person, you are able to contribute in a more valuable way to that relationship. For example, a couple where one spouse stays at home and the other goes to work every day would have to struggle with resentment if either of the spouses does not take the time to recognize the contributions of the other. And to recognize these contributions of the other person, one person would need to picture themselves in the shoes.

If the partner that does not see how difficult it is to manage the children at home and then keep the home in order, they would fail to appreciate the homeliness that they always come to meet at the end of their workday. And this is because they are more focused on the tedious activities they had to face in the office. This also goes vice versa. For couples in the same situation who empathize with each other, you would find them carrying out activities to make the life of their partners easier. The one who comes home from work would not immediately start requesting things; instead they look for areas where they can contribute to the upkeep of the home. And the same goes for the person who was at home. They would not make demands as soon as the other person comes home. Instead, they will give them space to allow them mentally decompress. This is what it means to empathize with people.

How Listening Can Help You See and Make Connections

When you have an emotional need or concern, you are most likely going to go to a person who you feel would listen to you. This also works with people in a relationship. They tend to air their views to people they feel will sympathize and listen to them. This often comes into play when we are thinking of the male and female dynamics in relationships. Men are not really talkers or great communicators are generally speaking in one on one relationships. They are actionable in nature and tend to be more of doers. Women, on the other hand, invest a lot in communicating their emotions and feelings.

The problem arises when the man feels that every time the woman says something, he has to do something about what she has said. But in reality, more often than not, what the woman needs is someone who would listen to what she is saying and sympathize with her. Listening, in this case, is not just about keeping your mouth shut and leaving your ears open. It goes beyond that. Earlier on, when I was talking about the art of small talk, I did say that one of the things you need to learn is how to actively listen and listening in this context also applies the same way.

You have to pay attention to what the person is saying so that you can hear them and then understand where they are coming from. It also helps you to empathize with the person. If you are able to actively listen to the people you are in a relationship with, you will find that you automatically become their confident. More than that, because you paid attention to what they are saying and you are able to understand and empathize with them, you are put in a better position to proffer solutions to their problems.

Everybody loves to be in a relationship with a problem solver and so it is important that you pay attention to what is being said. In the same vein, do not enter into every conversation with the intention to fix the other person because then every time they have a conversation with you, you would find it difficult to hear them out. This is most likely because you are already playing these scenarios in your head where you are fixing things.

You are not the human equivalent of correction fluid. It is ok if you don't fix a situation. Sometimes, all you need to do is just listen. Everything starts with active listening.

How to make them feel like your family

Family is one of those relationships in life that we have absolutely no control over. You do not choose who your biological relations are. You are basically born into them. However, when you start socializing, you are making a conscious decision to choose who you relate with and sometimes those relations that you build create a bond that can be likened to that of a family. The love, respect and loyalty in that relationship are enough to cement your bond for a long time. But how the people get from the point of being strangers to that place where they feel like this person they are with is a relationship for a lifetime? The main ingredients there is you. As I said earlier, when it comes to families, you have no choice in that matter. But in this situation, you are in complete control.

Without realizing it, we have been given the power to decide how long our relationships last. And before you try to make that argument, yes, it takes two or more to build a relationship. But it also comes from a conscious decision on your part. You would still need to be the one to apply certain principles and boundaries to enable that relationship to thrive. When you put a plant in soil, it is biologically programmed to grow. However, there are things you can do to ensure that the plant experiences excellent growth so that it is able to flourish and bear fruit. This phenomenon also applies to relationships. As humans, we are biologically programmed to connect with each other, but it requires effort on your part to foster and nurture that connection into a long-lasting relationship. When someone becomes your family, you are saying to that person that they are more than their flaws and mistakes. And that they have earned your loyalty and your trust and regardless of what happens in the future, you would always be there for them. There is also the unspoken expectation that they would also accept you in the same way.

I would like to insert here that it is important to ensure that the feeling is mutual. If not, you are setting yourself up for disappointment. Expectations have killed a lot of relationships mostly because we expect things that we can't give or we give things that we don't expect from the other person. There has to be a balance. If the relationship has that mutual feeling, the progression from the level of strangers to the family will take a natural turn. In fact, you probably would not even need to utter those words out loud. It is an unspoken commitment. My advice is this, you have been given an opportunity now to choose who you call family, apply due diligence in that process and most importantly, obey the golden rule of relationships; treat people as you expect to be treated.

The Difference Between Sincere and Fake

Let me start this segment by stating it categorically that if you are faking anything in a relationship, you have laid a foundation for dishonesty. A healthy relationship thrives on sincerity and openness. If there are areas where you have to fake communication and genuine affection for that person, I hate to be the one to break the news to you, but that is not a healthy relationship. If you have ever been at the receiving end of fake sincerity, you would understand how hurtful it is. There are people who manipulate their way into relationships to achieve a certain gain. For them, it is all about their goals and not about the needs of the person that they are in a relationship with. If this is you, I would advise you to desist from that. However, to prevent a situation where you are at the other end, here is how you can spot a fake from the real.

1. It feels too good to be true

Everybody wants to live in a fairytale and a lot of times, because of this idea that we have in our heads, we ignore signs that are glaring at us and focus on those things that we want in that relationship. So, instead of seeing the warning labels, we put on our rose-tinted glasses and ride on the highs that this relationship gives to us. If you find that everything appears to be perfect in your relationship, there is something missing. As I said earlier, relationships are not as complicated as we make it out to be; however, there are bound to be challenged. If yours is free from challenges and it is looking like it is straight out of a fairy tale novel, take a long pause and reevaluate that relationship.

2. You have a sense that something is wrong

Our instincts are designed to alert us to dangers or threats in our environment. In a relationship, if you get the sense that something is wrong, even though you just can't place your finger on it, there is a very strong possibility that something is actually wrong. You can either decide to become a Nancy Drew in that relationship and do some behind the scenes detective work or step back until you are able to figure things out. Either way, something is off and that is your instinct telling you that perhaps your relationship is lacking sincerity you desire.

3. Nobody around you seems to like this person

Now, this is a big red flag. No matter how unlikable a person may be, to an extent, you would still find people who would be rooting for them. However, if you find that the people with whom you share a close relationship within your life are unable to accept this new person, there is a chance that they see something that you cannot. And a lot of times, that thing that they are seeing is the insincerity of this person's actions.

Timing a Sincere Compliment and How to Insert it into the Flow of the Conversation

Complimenting someone in the conversation is a way of affirming your appreciation of the person with whom you are conversing with. However, you have to ensure that the compliment you are giving is appropriate to the circumstance. In a formal setting, for instance, you cannot make compliments about a person's body part. Even if they are about things that are innocent like their Eyes or nose. It would make the person feel uncomfortable and an awkward silence could ensue. Your component should be about a personality trait or their contribution to their profession.

Outside that, the next thing you need to focus on is how you deliver the compliment. You want the high praise that you are offering to the person to come off as natural as possible without seeming as though you have an ulterior motive. In my experience, I believe that the best way to achieve that is to avoid lingering on the compliment for too long, especially if you are in a crowded space. If you have a one on one conversation with the person, of course, you could go on to emphasize that particular compliment. However, you should also note that if that one on one conversation is being carried out in a formal setting, it is best to avoid lingering on that compliment. Simply say what you want to say in the most sincere way devoid of offensive words and then move on.

The art of the compliment (without sucking up to the other person)

For this part, I would say your intentions matter a lot. If you intend to suck up to a person, the compliments that you offer to them will actually come off as that sucking up. Because it would lack the genuineness that is required when offering compliments. Again, you should also avoid lingering on the compliments that you give or constantly repeating them. This is only appropriate when you are in a very close, informal relationship with a person. Perhaps, your friend or your romantic partner. In that scenario, I think you need to linger on your compliments as often and as long as you can.

Another mistake that people make when it comes to paying compliments to people is that they feel if you compliment a person, you cannot find something wrong with them. That is not true. It is possible that you like a person's display of empathy; however, you may have a problem with how intense they are in those moments. And because you care about this person, you call them out on it. In healthy relationships, whether formal or informal, genuine compliments go hand-in-hand with constructive criticisms. If you find that you are unable to criticize a person even though you see glaring things that they are doing wrong, but you constantly find yourself complimenting them, it is safe to say that you are sucking up to them.

Chapter Eleven

Social Interactions in a Group Setting

Now, we have come to the moment of truth. In the previous chapters, we looked at initiating conversations with people one on one as well as inserting yourself into groups. Now, we are going to take things a step further. We are no longer looking at establishing a relationship with one person. We are looking at how you can carry a group along. And in this context, I am not just going to focus on networking in groups. I would look at you being a public speaker. I know that for an introvert, this is a giant leap, but that is how much faith I have in you. Because if I was able to go from being this shy kid to this person who is always excited to get on stage, I believe that so can you.

Group Conversation Flow

In a group conversation, three things can happen. You are either under the spotlight, which means you are the main person championing the conversation. Or you could be a spectator, which means that you are the one who listens more than you speak. Then you have the last situation, which I feel is the most ideal situation; you are sharing the spotlight with all the people in the group. To ensure that you are not lost in that group conversation, the first thing you need to do is identify what role you are playing.

Are you going to be in the spotlight? If you are under the spotlight, it means that you have to be the one leading the conversation, and by leading the conversation, it does not necessarily mean that you are the only one talking. Remember what I said about great conversationalists. They don't take control of the conversation. Somehow, they are able to immerse themselves in the conversation and still give everyone the room to express themselves. If you would rather play the role of the listener, you need to be an active listener. And that means you pay attention to what is being said. Understand what the person is saying and where they are coming from and then interject occasionally with questions based on the information you have received. Try as much as possible not to go off point

And finally, if you are in the last scenario where everyone is sharing the spotlight, the key to balancing it is to be both the listener and the person under the spotlight. You listen to people talking, get their point of view and then assert yourself in the conversation. There are people who have a tendency to want to talk you down. It is your responsibility to take control of your own voice. Not by increasing the pitch of your voice but by ensuring that you assert yourself. That way, you are making yourself heard and are actively contributing to the flow of the conversation.

How to Join an Existing Group Conversation

Unless you are aiming for drama, I will suggest that you enter the group as quietly as possible. And then before you make a speech, listen to what is being said. Hear the views and opinions of the people that are talking in that group and then based on the information that you get; you can then ask a question. Be warned, though; do not go into the conversation with your guns blazing. That spreads hostility and may make the people in that group feel a little bit resentful of you. Even though your point may be just what they need to get the conversation going, you need to take the gentle approach.

As you continue contributing to that conversation, you can take off your gloves and then get into it really deep. The reason I asked that you delay a little before asserting yourself is so that you are able to get your bearings. Understand what the conversation is about, know where most of the people in that group stand regarding the conversation and then assert yourself to make your own contribution. When you listen, you are able to understand more and when you understand more, you are less likely going to make a fool of yourself.

This is after all our biggest fears when we get into conversations that involve groups of people.

Group Conversation Guidelines and Principles for Standing Out and Making a Connection

This here is where you learn the art of public speaking. I understand that right now you are not a public speaker, and you probably have no intention of becoming one. But at some point in your life, you may be called upon to address a group of at least ten people. If you start practicing and preparing yourself for that moment, when that time comes, you will find that you are able to have a conversation with your crowd easily and you would do this without fretting or panicking.

The key thing there is to apply everything you have learned so far. But instead of focusing on just one person, focus on the group in the room. The technique I usually use is to have the mindset that I am talking to one person but act as though I am communicating with the group. So, I try as much as possible to use the space that is available to me. For instance, if you are standing on an elevated podium, staying still in one spot does not really help you engage your crowd. You need to take a few steps at a time and keep your eyes on the crowd. You can choose a certain spot to concentrate your gaze on. Occasionally and from time-to-time, let your gaze go over the people in the other parts of the room.

Be as animated as possible in your conversation. Let your hand gestures be appropriate but do not standstill. And finally, put everything you have learned on the art of storytelling to good use. Be clear in whatever message you are trying to pass across. Let it have its starting point in a story and the story should be something that your audience can relate with. Also remember, language is important. Speak in a language that the crowd will understand and avoid the use of offensive words. For this last part, pretend as though your very existence is dependent on it. Because offending one person in a one on one conversation is bad enough. To do it in a group, that could spell the end of your career and affect your ability to speak in public.

And with that, we have come to the end of this book. But don't close it yet, I still have a few words to share with you.

Conclusion

Once again, I am so proud of how far you have come on this journey, and I am deeply honored that I was involved (even if it was in the tiniest way) to help you overcome your social anxiety and become a better version of yourself. Relationships are important. No matter the lies we tell ourselves because of our hurts and past experiences, we still need people around us. With this in mind, I would like you to subscribe to the knowledge that you are in control of the relationships that you develop in your life. You may not be able to control the actions that people take. However, you have a strong voice in determining the kind of people who stay in your life and those who don't.

Going forward, I want you to develop this mindset as you deal with people. Not everybody has to be your best friend and not everybody has to like you. You are important as a person and you deserve to be treated as though you are important. So, choose people who choose you. Treat people the way you want to be treated. You do not deserve anything less. We may have come to the end of this book but believe me when I say that your journey is just beginning. And if you can step outside of your comfort zone, I can guarantee you that life outside your door is going to be exciting and fun. There is nothing to be scared of.

Even when people tell you 'no,' that word carries a blessing. That 'no' is basically sparing you from the heartache of what the relationship would have been if they said 'yes.' And so, rejection is not the ultimate definition of your life. Some of the people you encounter would choose to walk away from you. That is ok, in my opinion, perfect even. Your mantra going forward should be "***choose people who choose me***." I wish you all the best in your professional and social life. And I hope that from this book, you are able to become better at communication and for that reason, you are able to build better relationships. Please remember to pay it forward by passing the knowledge you have gained here to other people in your shoes.

From me and everyone who contributed to making this book a success, we are sending love, light and laughter to you.

www.ingramcontent.com/pod-product-compliance
Lightning Source LLC
Chambersburg PA
CBHW051736020426
42333CB00014B/1335